CW01221112

Written by
ANNA CLAYBOURNE

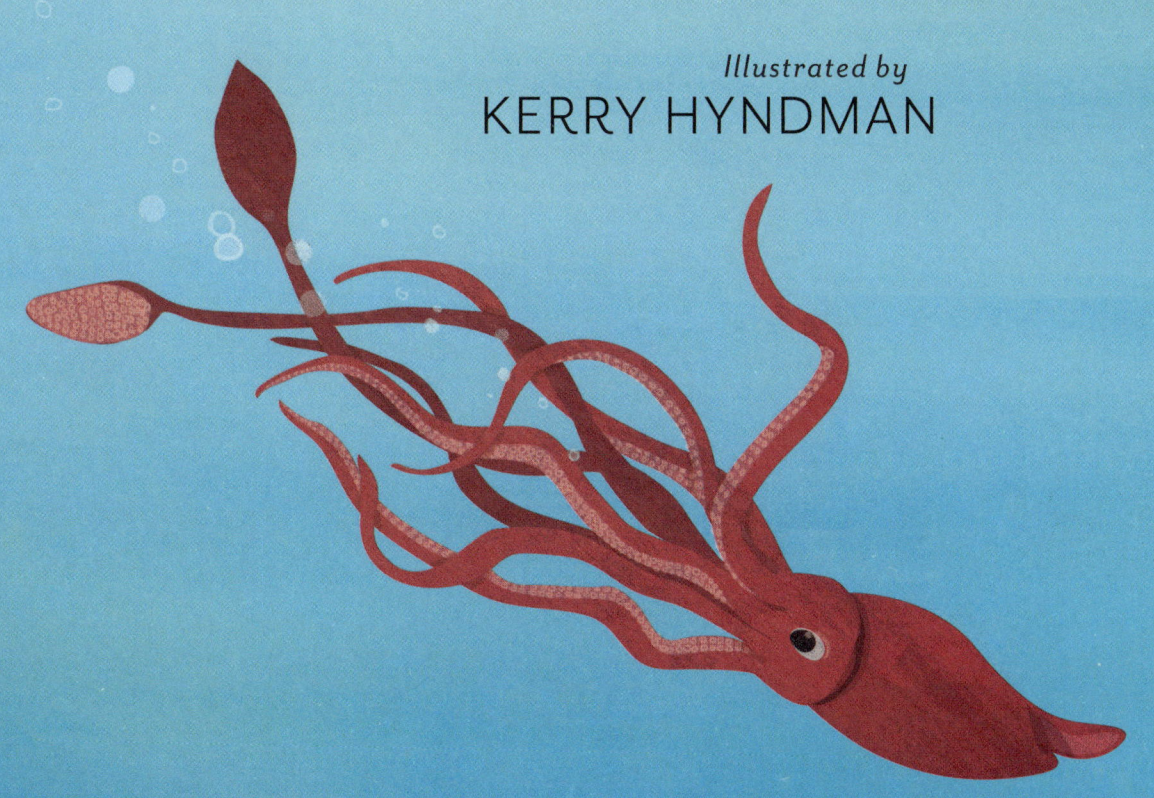

WATERWORLDS

Illustrated by
KERRY HYNDMAN

Published in 2024 by Welbeck Children's
An imprint of Hachette Children's Group,
Part of Hodder & Stoughton Limited
Carmelite House, 50 Victoria Embankment
London EC4Y 0DZ

An Hachette UK Company
www.hachette.co.uk
www.hachettechildrens.co.uk

Text © 2025 Hachette Children's Group
Illustration © 2025 Kerry Hyndman

Kerry Hyndman has asserted their moral rights to be identified as the illustrator of this Work in accordance with the Copyright Designs and Patents Act 1988.

All rights reserved. No part of this publication may be reproduced, stored in a retrieval system, or transmitted in any form or by any means, electronically, mechanical, photocopying, recording or otherwise, without the prior permission of the copyright owners and the publishers.

A CIP catalogue record for this book is available from the British Library.

HB ISBN: 978-1-803-38142-8
E-book ISBN: 978-1-804-53764-0

Printed in China

1 3 5 7 9 10 8 6 4 2

(p21) Monopoly® is a registered trademark of Hasbro, Inc.

CONTENTS

Under the sea — 4
Salty seas — 6
Underwater stories — 8
Going down . . . — 10
Fish in the sea — 12
The deepest depths — 14
The deep seabed — 16
Sea monsters — 18
Shipwrecks — 20
Exploring the deep — 22
Underwater journeys — 24
Oceans in danger — 26
Undersea forests — 28
Coral reefs — 30
Leaping out — 32

Under the sea

What lies beneath the waves that ruffle the surface of the seas and oceans? A huge, mysterious, hidden realm, much of it still unexplored. In some places, the water is shallow enough to wade in. But in others, it's so deep you could stand Mount Everest on the seabed and seawater would cover the summit.

As you sink down deeper and deeper, the sea gets colder and darker, guarding its strange secrets and curious creatures. In this watery world lives a vast variety of life, from swirling seaweeds and hot-water-loving worms to snapping shrimp, schools of fish so big they contain billions, and huge, far-wandering whales. There may be other life forms too, still unknown to science, living deep beneath the waves and waiting to be discovered.

Salty seas

If you've ever got seawater in your mouth, you'll know it tastes salty and is not good to drink. But why is the sea full of salt, when streams, rivers and lakes aren't?

Dissolved rocks

As streams and rivers run, they dissolve tiny amounts of chemicals from the rocks they flow past. The chemicals get carried into the sea.

Thanks to the water cycle (flip the book and turn to page 6), water also leaves the sea, by evaporating into a gas and floating up into the sky. But when this happens, the dissolved chemicals get left behind.

Some of the chemicals get used by sea creatures, for example to make their shells. But others don't, so, over time, they build up. Table salt, or sodium chloride, is the most common one, and makes up three per cent of seawater – which is why it has a salty taste.

As well as the salt, there are much smaller amounts of other minerals dissolved in seawater too, including: magnesium, calcium, iron, zinc, mercury, silver. And even gold!

The salt in seawater makes it more dense, or heavy for its size, and this means it's easier to float in than fresh (non-salty) water.

Sea creatures like this whelk use calcium, a mineral in seawater, to make their shells.

Salt from the sea

We can collect salt from seawater to use in cooking. To do this, salt harvesters put seawater in shallow pools in the sunshine. The water evaporates, leaving crunchy salt crystals behind.

Too much salt!

When fish get thirsty, they have to drink seawater – but just like us, it's too salty for them. Their bodies filter the salt out and it comes out in their wee – back into the sea.

Marine iguanas are the only sea-diving lizards. The salty seawater is bad for their bodies too, but they have special salt glands that collect the salt in their noses. Then, back on land, they sneeze the salt out!

COLLECT SALT CRYSTALS

Try this easy experiment to see how salt gets left behind when water evaporates.

YOU NEED:
A tablespoon of cooking salt
A cup or mug
Hot tap water
A saucer

1. Ask an adult to half-fill the cup or mug with hot tap water.

2. Add the tablespoon of salt, and stir. Keep stirring for at least two minutes to dissolve as much of the salt as possible.

3. Put your saucer in a warm place, such as a sunny windowsill.

4. Put a few tablespoons of the salty water in the saucer.

5. Leave it for a day, or until the water has all gone. You should be left with white, crunchy salt crystals.

Underwater stories

What magical wonders lurk beneath the waves? Since ancient times, myths and legends have told of strange half-human sea creatures and ocean gods and goddesses, and their other-worldly underwater homes.

Magical mermaids

Mermaids are half-human, with a fish's tail instead of legs, and they are found in folklore from all over the world. They're often female, but there are also mermen. Some merfolk can be scary, luring sailors to a watery grave, or coming ashore to steal a human husband or wife. Others can be helpful, sending good weather and shoals of fish for seafarers, or singing to warn humans of a coming storm.

In North American Mi'kmaq mythology, the Sabawaelnu, or Halfway People, are small merfolk. Their songs can protect people from danger at sea – but if you don't show them enough respect, they might summon up a storm.

In northern Scotland, blue-skinned, green-bearded mermen called the Blue Men of the Minch are said to live in a stretch of sea called the Minch, famous for its storms. When the Blue Men sleep in their undersea caves, all is calm, but when they swim and dive at the surface, they whip up the waves and can sink boats and ships.

Jiaoren are kind, beautiful mermaids from Chinese folklore. They weave delicate sea silk fabric and play underwater flutes, and their tears become precious pearls. If a Jiaoren gives you one of her pearls as a gift, you will gain the power to breathe underwater.

Underwater dwellings

Many ocean gods, goddesses and monsters have their own undersea homes. Ryujin, the dragon king of the sea in Japanese legends, dwells in a place of red and pink coral at the bottom of the sea. Sometimes, so the stories say, humans have been able to visit it – but for every year they spend there, 100 years go by on land.

Ancient Greek sea god Triton was also said to live in a palace under the sea, where he kept his hippocampi, or fish-tailed mer-horses.

Sunken lands

There are many legends of ancient lands, towns or palaces that disappeared beneath the waves. Atlantis, a perfect island city described by the ancient Greeks, was said to have sunk under the sea, and people have been searching for it ever since.

There's still no evidence Atlantis ever existed, but some legends of buildings under the sea could be based on fact. For many centuries, legends told how Mahabalipuram in India had seven beautiful temples, but six were flooded by the sea, leaving just one on the shore. In 2002, divers discovered the ruins of temple-like buildings on the seabed.

INTERTIDAL ZONE, *between high and low tide*

Sailfish

Turtle

Dolphin

Going down...

Near the surface of the sea, sunlight filters through the water, and there's lots of wildlife around. But the deeper you go, the darker it gets, and the more pressure there is from the weight of all the water above you.

Cuvier's beaked whale

Different kinds of sea creatures live at different depths. Some move from one zone to another – for example, Cuvier's beaked whale breathes air at the surface, but can dive down into the midnight zone to hunt for fish.

Viperfish

Snailfish

Sea spider

Ocean zones

Scientists divide the seas and oceans into five different depth zones. They don't all exist everywhere – in many places, the sea isn't deep enough to include all five zones. In this picture, though, you can see them all.

Trench, an extra-deep channel or dip in the sea bed

Amphipods

Drifting around

Near the surface, plankton flows and drifts this way and that with the waves, tides and currents. It's a mixture of many types of small or microscopic living things, such as algae, tiny shrimps and worms, and the larvae or babies of sea creatures like starfish and jellyfish. They provide food for countless other sea creatures.

Giant squid

Gulper eel

Submersible

In the deep sea, the water pressure is so great that no human can survive, unless they're safely inside a super-strong submersible.

0 m

SUNLIGHT OR EPIPELAGIC ZONE
lit by sunlight

200 m

TWILIGHT OR MESOPELAGIC ZONE
with very little light

1,000 m

MIDNIGHT OR BATHYPELAGIC ZONE
where it's very dark

4,000 m

ABYSSAL OR ABYSSOPELAGIC ZONE
deep, dark and cold

6,000 m

HADAL OR HADOPELAGIC ZONE
found in deep trenches

11,000 m
that's as deep as the ocean gets!

Sardines swim in ginormous shoals.

Ocean sunfish
This huge fish lacks a tail.

Fish in the sea

There are 20,000 different types, or species, of fish in the seas and oceans, from teeny infantfish to giant sharks. And how many fish are there in total? Scientists think the answer is at least 3.5 TRILLION – that's 3.5 million million, or 3,500,000,000,000.

What is a fish?

Fish are animals with gills for breathing underwater. Most fish also have fins, a tail, and scaly skin, but there are other types too. Sharks, for example, have rough spiky skin, and eels and hagfish have no fins (or very small ones) and look more like snakes. You can see the main parts of a fish on this snowy grouper, an Atlantic Ocean fish.

This line is called the **lateral line**. It senses vibrations and pressure in the water, helping the fish to feel its own movement and detect other animals moving nearby.

Dorsal fin

Some fish have back spines too

Gill cover

Eye

Nostril

Tail, used for swimming

Fins

Water flows into a fish's mouth and out through the gills on the sides of its neck. In the gills, blood vessels soak up dissolved oxygen from the water.

Most fish are 'bony fish', and have skeletons made of bone.

Leafy sea dragon A fish covered in leafy camouflage, not a dragon!

Seahorse A fish that swims upright, with a horse-shaped head.

Red-lipped batfish use their feet-shaped fins to walk on the seabed.

Flounders can change colour to blend in with their surroundings.

12

The biggest fish in the world is the **whale shark**, which grows up to 12 metres long.

Hammerhead shark
Its wide-apart eyes help it to look around for prey.

Ocellated ray

Sharks and rays belong to a separate group, the cartilaginous fish. Their skeletons are mostly made of tough, rubbery cartilage, making them more flexible.

Pufferfish puff themselves up into a spiky ball to put off predators.

Hagfish belong to a group called the jawless fish. They have no fins, and burrow into dead sea creatures to feed on them.

The **stout infantfish** is the smallest of all sea fish, at just eight millimetres long!

Actual size!

Lionfish

NOT A FISH!

Quite a few sea creatures have 'fish' in their name but are not fish at all . . .

Jellyfish
– actually a cnidarian, with no bones or brain

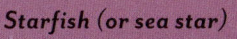

Starfish (or sea star)
– an echinoderm

Cuttlefish
– a mollusc, related to octopuses and squid

Shellfish
– molluscs with shells, such as mussels

The deepest depths

What lives in the deep, dark ocean, where no sunlight from above can reach? Fish and other sea creatures here often have their own lights, to lure prey towards them or help them find a mate. Some of them look quite scary too...

Gulper or pelican eel

Its huge lower jaw can expand to swallow prey even bigger than itself!

Deep sea fish

These fearsome and strange fish lurk in the deep, dark ocean. Though they can look frightening, most of them are quite small!

Goblin shark

This odd-looking deep-sea shark is soft and flabby, with a long snout and jaws that stick out to grab food.

*A **Pacific viperfish** has fangs so big, they can't fit inside its mouth.*

Humpback anglerfish

Anglerfish have a glowing lure on their heads, to attract smaller animals towards their huge fang-filled mouths.

Creepy creatures
Many other sea creatures prowl the deep ocean too . . .

Glass octopus
See-through body

Vampire squid have glowing tips on their tentacles, and can squirt out glowing ink to distract hunters.

Not many octopuses can glow with their own light, but these two deep-sea species can.

Deep sea crown jelly, a glowing jellyfish

Glowing sucker octopus

Green bomber worms throw out glowing green balls to send predators in the wrong direction.

THE ISLAND OF GUAM, the nearest land

MARIANA TRENCH

CHALLENGER DEEP

Amphipod

Sea cucumber

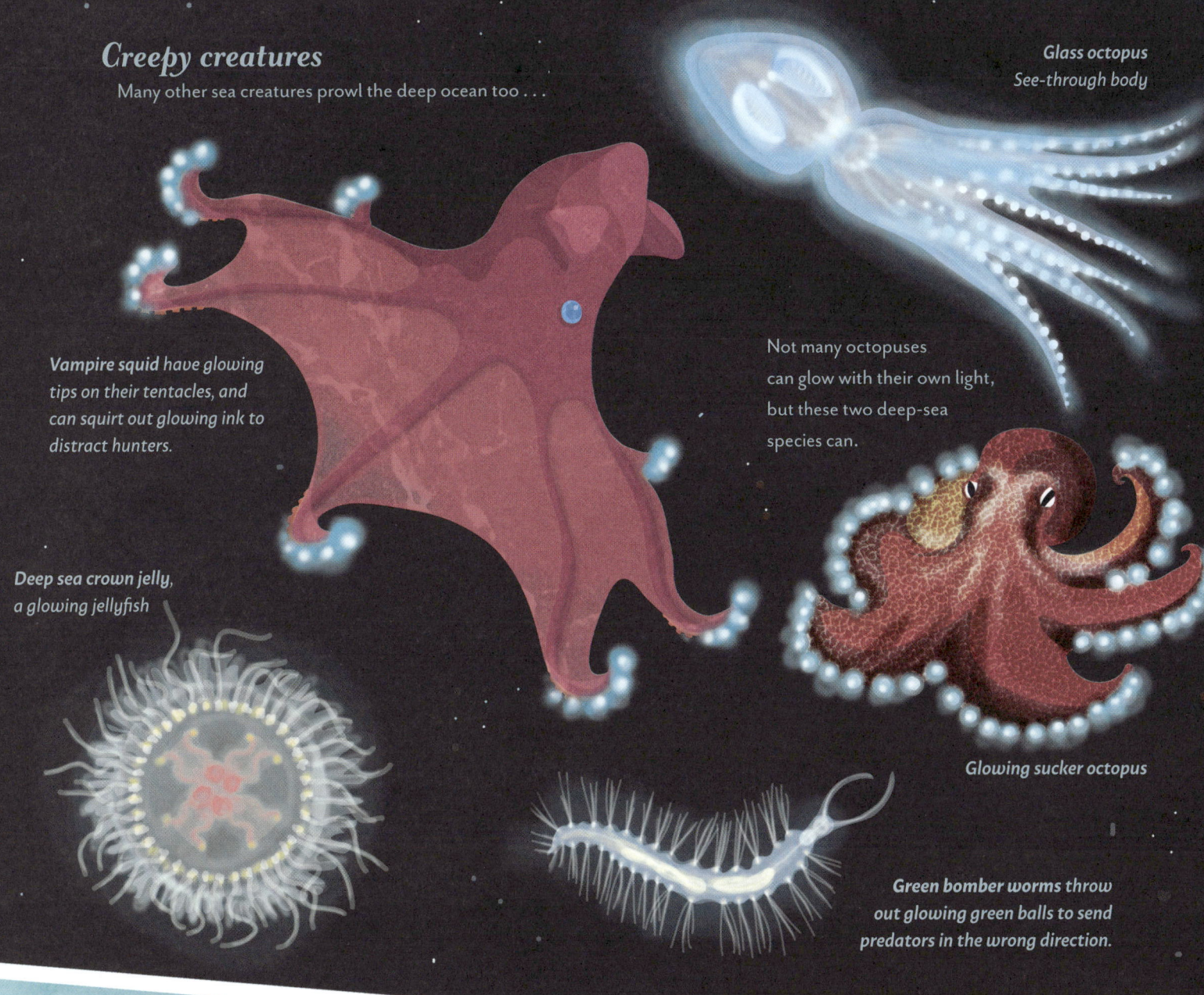

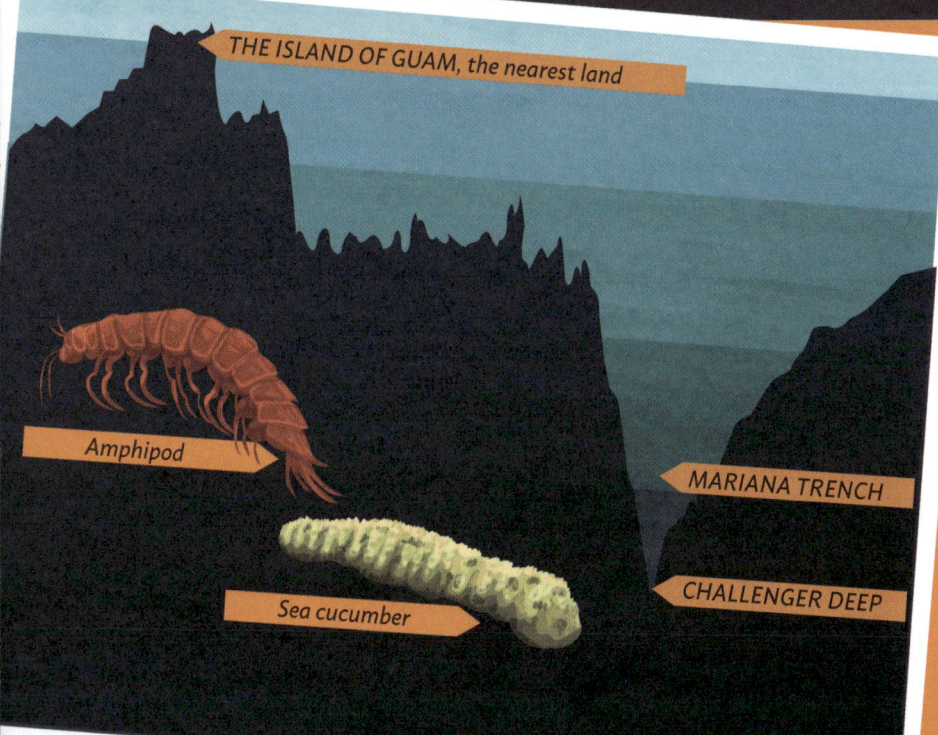

How low can you go?
The deepest point in all the world's oceans is Challenger Deep, part of the Mariana Trench in the western Pacific Ocean, south of Japan. It's about 10,924 metres, or almost 11 kilometres deep. Humans have visited the deepest point several times, in deep-sea submersibles.

Even this deep, some sea creatures survive, such as amphipods (tiny shrimp-like animals) and sea cucumbers (which are actually animals related to starfish, not cucumbers!). There are no plants, as they need light to live, and the deep sea is pitch black.

The deep seabed

Down at the bottom of the ocean is the abyssal plain, or deep seabed. It's a dark and gloomy world of slime and strange creatures, with constantly falling snow – though not the kind of snow we're used to . . .

Who lives here?

Many of the animals that live here feed on the ooze, crawling or slithering over it. Others swim just above the ocean floor.

Sea spiders

Sea spiders are related to land spiders, but can have up to 12 legs, and are often much bigger. They can swim or tiptoe over the ooze, and feed on other animals like sea anemones.

Tripod spiderfish

This strange fish uses its long fins like a tripod to perch on the ooze, then snaps up smaller animals that swim past.

Deep sea urchin

Sea cucumbers

Sea cucumbers are animals related to starfish. This one, known as the 'gummy squirrel', sifts through the sediment with its tentacles to collect food.

Dumbo octopus

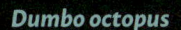

This octopus gets its name from its two fins that look like elephant ears. It hovers just above the seabed, hunting for worms and other small animals to eat.

Marine snow

Marine snow (meaning sea snow) is made of millions of bits of waste drifting down onto the seabed from higher up in the ocean. It includes dead plankton and other small sea creatures, fish scales, bits of food dropped by animals, animal poop, and mucus (or animal snot). It also contains mud, sand and bits of seashell and coral.

As the snow settles, it covers the seabed in soft, slimy sediment called 'ooze', making it flat and smooth.

High-speed signals

There's something more modern down here too: huge cables, thousands of kilometres long, snaking across the deep ocean floor. They carry internet signals and messages from one continent to another.

Scotoplanes

Scotoplanes or 'sea pigs' are another type of sea cucumber. Sometimes they gather in huge 'herds', snuffling in the ooze for food.

Isopod

The giant isopod is a relative of woodlice, growing to 50 cm long. It nibbles the bodies of dead animals that sink onto the ocean floor, such as whales and sharks.

Sea monsters

Since ancient times, sailors have told thrilling tales of terrifying sea monsters, so big they could sink ships. Were they just tall stories... or could they have been descriptions of real creatures of the deep?

The Kraken

This scary sea monster from Scandinavian folklore was said to be a giant water beast with many arms or tentacles. It would burst out of the sea, entangle itself around a ship and drag it under the surface, before devouring the entire crew.
It was also said to float at the surface, where it would attract shoals of fish. Brave fishing crews would sometimes venture near a kraken to scoop up an easy catch.

COULD IT HAVE BEEN...

A giant squid — or something even bigger?

With its big eyes and powerful tentacles, the Kraken may have been based on sightings of the giant squid or colossal squid. They can grow to 13 or 14 m long, including the arms. Giant squid have been known to chase and attack boats, although they don't sink them. But maybe, somewhere in the ocean depths, there's an even BIGGER squid — a monster-sized one — waiting to be discovered.

The Sea Serpent

Giant sea serpents of folklore are huge scaly, snake-shaped monsters that lurk in the ocean and snatch sailors from the decks of ships. They appear in folklore around the world.

The Living Island, or Aspidochelone

In several ancient travellers' tales, sailors land their boat on what seems to be a small uninhabited island. They explore and light a fire. That's when they discover that the island is alive! Feeling the heat, it starts to writhe and roar, then plunges below the waves, taking the sailors with it. It's usually described as either a giant turtle, or a giant whale.

COULD IT HAVE BEEN...

COULD IT HAVE BEEN...

One of these?

Sea serpent stories could have arisen from sailors spotting something like this...

An oarfish, a huge silver snake-shaped fish with a dragon-like head.

A blue whale, or Archelon?

The blue whale is not only the world's biggest whale, but the biggest animal that's ever lived – even bigger than the biggest dinosaurs – at up to 30 m long. When its back surfaces above the water, it could look a bit like an island. There's no turtle this big, but millions of years ago, the giant turtle Archelon roamed the seas. Perhaps something like it – or an even bigger turtle – has secretly survived...

Or a giant pyrosome, a glowing tube up to 10 m long, made of tiny animals called zooids that live together in a group, or colony.

Shipwrecks

On seabeds all over the world lie the remains of sunken ships. Some are hundreds or even thousands of years old. Many lie in shallow water, where they sank after crashing into rocks or sandbanks. Others rest on the deep seabed, after sinking in a storm, or, like the famous ocean liner *Titanic*, crashing into an iceberg.

Gribble

Shipworm

Sea change

After a boat or ship sinks, it begins to change...

Wooden planks and cabins start to decay and rot. Sea creatures such as shipworms and gribbles burrow into them and eat them away.

Shipworms are relatives of sea snails, and use their sharp shells to bore into wood.

Gribbles are tiny isopods, related to shrimps and crabs.

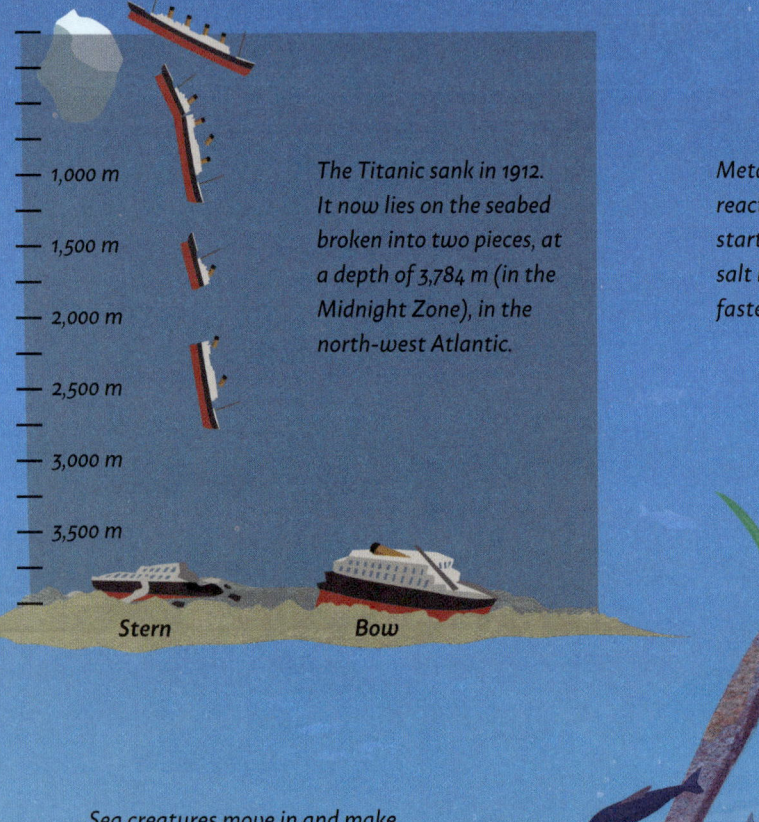

1,000 m
1,500 m
2,000 m
2,500 m
3,000 m
3,500 m

The Titanic sank in 1912. It now lies on the seabed broken into two pieces, at a depth of 3,784 m (in the Midnight Zone), in the north-west Atlantic.

Stern   Bow

Metal parts, especially iron and steel, react with oxygen in the water. They start to oxidise and turn into rust. The salt in the seawater makes this happen faster than on land.

Corals start growing on the wreck.

Sea creatures move in and make the wreck their home.

Sunken treasure

Not all sunken ships contain treasure, but some do. In the 1500s, 1600s and 1700s, sailing ships carried stolen gold and silver from the Americas to Europe, while pirate ships chased and raided them. These ships sometimes sank, taking their loot down with them. People sometimes try to salvage or retrieve the treasure, but a lot of it is still on the seabed.

After hundreds of years underwater, copper and silver coins look tarnished and discoloured. But gold coins stay bright and shiny, as they don't react with the seawater.

Scuba divers explore old wrecks under the water.

Sea anemones, sponges and seaweeds find places to anchor themselves.

The coral-encrusted wreck provides food and shelter for other animals too, such as crabs, octopuses and parrotfish.

SHIPWRECK COINS

Use this simple method to make normal copper coins look as if they've been at the bottom of the sea for centuries.

YOU NEED:
A few copper coins
A plate
Kitchen paper
Salt
Vinegar

1. Put the paper on the plate, then put the coins on top.
2. Sprinkle the paper and coins with vinegar.
3. Then sprinkle the coins with salt, and leave somewhere safe for 24 hours.

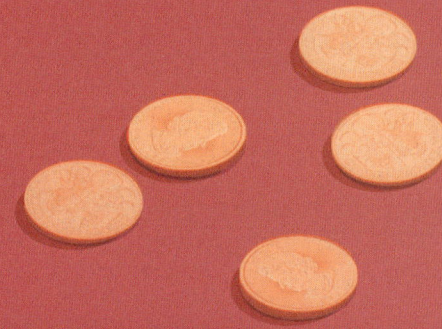

The vinegar cleans the coins, and the salt helps the copper to react with oxygen in the air.

This makes a green coating.

Exploring the deep

As humans don't have gills and can only breathe air, it's hard for us to dive deep under the seas and oceans. But we've invented all kinds of things to help us do it . . .

Ancient diving

Before modern inventions, people had to hold their breath to dive into the sea. They went diving to collect seafood, or precious pearls, which grow in oyster shells.

Over 2,000 years ago, the ancient Greeks were using diving bells to explore underwater. A diving bell is a heavy bell-shaped shelter that is lowered into the water, trapping air inside. Divers can leave the bell for a short time, then come back in for air – but the fresh air doesn't last for very long.

Submarines

Submarines, or underwater boats, have been around for hundreds of years. An early sub from the 1600s was powered by oars! Since then, we've used submarines for exploring, studying the seabed, war and tourism.

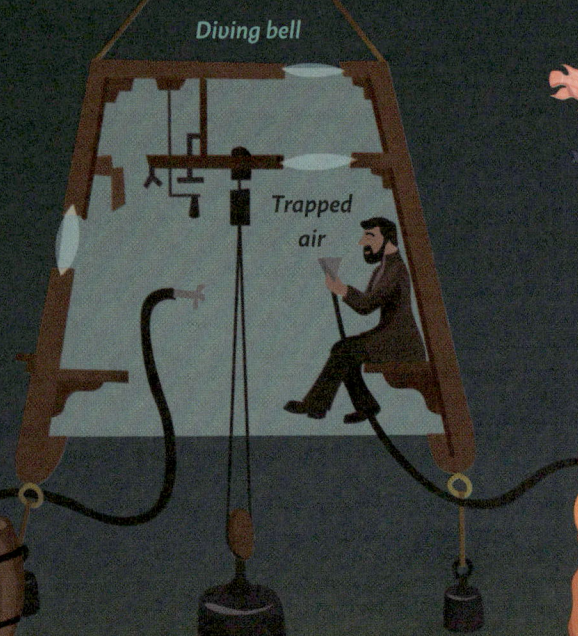

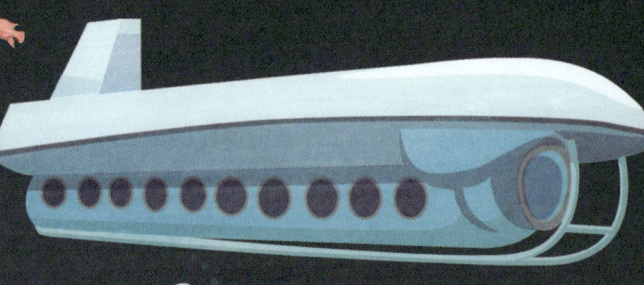

Diving bell

Trapped air

A modern tourist sub for undersea wildlife-watching.

Snorkels and SCUBA

For a continuous air supply, you can use a snorkel – a breathing tube that sticks out above the water surface. They have been used for thousands of years too.

In the 1900s, a new invention called SCUBA (Self-Contained Underwater Breathing Apparatus) made it possible to go on longer, deeper dives, breathing from a tank of compressed air.

Breathing tube

Air tank

Goggles

Breathing tube

Flippers

Down to the depths

To dive to the deep ocean, explorers and scientists use smaller submarines called submersibles. In 1977, scientists exploring in a submersible named Alvin discovered hydrothermal vents, where hot, mineral-filled water flows out from under the seabed. Unusual animals live around the vents in the hot water.

Vent octopus

Giant tube worms

Vent crab

BOTTLE DIVER

To move up and down, submarines use ballast tanks full of air. To sink, water is added to the tank, squeezing the air into a smaller space and making the sub heavier.

You can make a diver that works the same way in this experiment.

YOU NEED:
A large clear plastic drinks bottle with a lid
A pen lid like this, with a clip on the side, and no hole in the top
Modelling clay or sticky tack
A cup
Water

1. Make a ball of clay or sticky tack and stick it to the pen lid clip.

2. As a test, fill the cup with water and put the lid in, clip end down. Adjust the amount of clay until the pen lid only just floats.

3. Fill the bottle with water to the brim, put the pen lid in the top, and screw the lid on tightly.

4. Now use both hands to squeeze the bottle.

When you do, the pen lid should dive! Squeezing the bottle pushes some water into the pen lid, squashing the air, so the pen lid sinks. Let go, and it will go up again.

Underwater journeys

We can roam all over the seas and oceans by boat, and sea creatures can do the same underwater. Some of them journey thousands of kilometres across oceans or around the world.

Pacific Ocean

Indonesia

Australia

Turtle travels

Leatherback turtles are great migrators, swimming from nesting beaches in the tropics to cooler feeding areas where they hunt jellyfish. Using a tracker fitted to a leatherback, scientists found it made a journey of over 20,000 km, across the Pacific from Indonesia to the northwestern USA.

WHY IS THERE MORE FOOD IN COLD WATER?

It might seem strange that sea creatures head to colder waters to feed, but that's because they are full of food. Cold water can hold more dissolved oxygen, helping more plankton and other sea life to live there. And near the poles, the sun shines all night in summer, making it easier for algae to grow. It feeds small animals, and they become food for bigger creatures like whales.

Krill feed on algae.

North America

Atlantic Ocean

Central America

Wandering whales

Humpback whales, like many other large whales, migrate long distances between their favourite feeding areas around the North and South Poles, and their breeding grounds near the equator.

When winter comes, humpbacks migrate to warmer tropical waters around Central America to breed.

South America

A female humpback is pregnant for 11 months, so she goes to spend the summer feeding in the Antarctic, then returns to give birth.

The distance is around 8,000 km one-way. In a 40–year lifespan, a humpback could travel over 600,000 km, or 15 times around the world.

After giving birth, she migrates back to Antarctica, this time with her baby, or calf, beside her.

When it's summer in Antarctica, some humpbacks go there to feed on small fish, and shrimp-like animals called krill.

Southern Ocean

25

Oceans in danger

The sea and oceans are changing, thanks to global warming and other problems caused by humans. This makes life harder for a lot of ocean species.

Pacific Ocean

Asia

Overfishing

Humans have fished in the seas and oceans for thousands of years, but if we catch too many of one species, they can become endangered. The ornate eagle ray is one of many shark and ray species endangered by overfishing.

Indian Ocean

In Indonesia, pollution from nickel mines can turn the sea red and kill fish.

Australia

Acid oceans

Burning fuel in vehicles and power stations releases extra carbon dioxide into the air. Some gets dissolved in the seas and oceans, and that turns seawater into a weak acid. The acidic water dissolves and weakens some sea creatures' shells.

ENDANGERED SPECIES

As well as sharks and rays, these sea species are now endangered:

Leatherback turtle
Affected by pollution, global warming and egg collecting

Nassau grouper
Affected by overfishing

The Great Pacific Garbage Patch is a mass of plastic rubbish, three times the size of France, floating in the Pacific Ocean.

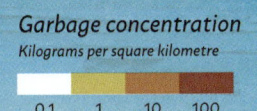

Garbage concentration
Kilograms per square kilometre

0.1   1   10   100

North America

Atlantic Ocean

Warming waters

The extra carbon dioxide in the air traps heat and makes the world warmer. Warmer water can harm or kill some kinds of sea life.

Pollution

Pollution is dirt or waste that escapes into the environment. Because the seas and oceans lie in the lowest parts of the Earth's crust, pollution often ends up being washed into them from the land, or flowing into them along rivers.

Chemicals from farms, factories and mines flow into the sea, especially after heavy rain.

Sewage (waste from sinks and toilets) should get cleaned up, but sometimes it flows straight into the sea too. Lots of litter ends up in the sea as well.

South America

Coral polyps are the tiny sea creatures that build coral reefs. When they get too warm, they lose algae that live in their bodies and provide them with food. This turns them white and makes them weaker – an effect called coral bleaching.

Sea creatures can die from eating litter. For example, some sea turtles eat plastic bags, maybe because they look like jellyfish, and this can block their stomachs.

Chambered nautilus
Affected by being overfished for its shell

Short-nosed sea snake
Affected by warmer seas and being accidentally caught in fishing nets

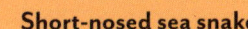

Vaquita porpoise
Gets caught in fishing nets

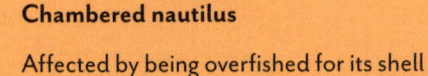

Undersea forests

Close to the coast, seaweeds and sea plants soak up the sunlight that shines through the shallow water. In some places, kelp seaweed grows in huge, greenish-brown forests that sway with the waves. Like forests on land, they provide a home and food for other wildlife.

Trees of the sea

At the bottom, kelp has parts called holdfasts that anchor it to rocks on the seabed. The rest of the leafy seaweed reaches up towards the sunlit surface, sometimes growing over 50 metres tall.

The ringed top snail feeds on the blades, or leaves, of kelp.

Sea otters dive down to hunt sea urchins, crabs and shellfish, then take them up to the surface to eat.

Rockfish

Sunflower sea stars live on the sea bed and hunt other animals.

Purple sea urchins feed on the kelp holdfasts.

Grey whales use the thick kelp to hide from hungry orcas.

Garibaldi fish

Northern kelp crab

SEAWEED CHIPS

Seaweed is a food for humans too. It's used around the world as a vegetable, and to make salads, sushi and snacks. To make seaweed chips, you need some nori seaweed sheets from a supermarket (and an adult to help!).

YOU NEED:
1 pack of seaweed sheets
Olive oil or other cooking oil
Salt

1. Heat the oven to 150 ° C or gas mark 2.
2. Brush a baking tray with oil.
3. Cut the seaweed sheets into snack-sized squares or triangles and lay them on the tray.
4. Brush more oil on top.
5. Bake in the oven for about 5-10 minutes, until crispy, and leave to cool.

UNDERWATER MEADOWS

As well as forests, there are meadows under the sea, made of seagrass, an underwater plant similar to land grass. There are even cows – sea cows, or dugongs. These large sea mammals graze on the seagrass with their big, flattened snouts.

Coral reefs

In the shallowest, sunniest parts of the sea, in warm tropical waters, you can find the colourful underwater world of the coral reef. Like a kelp forest, coral provides shelter, food and a habitat (or home) for other sea creatures – but it comes from a very different kind of living thing.

What is coral?

Coral is similar to seashell. It's a hard substance that sea creatures called coral polyps make to live in. But instead of each having their own separate shells, the coral polyps live together in big groups, and they and their coral are all linked.

Saltwater crocodiles often swim in the sea, and hunt fish and turtles on coral reefs.

Coral polyps are tiny relatives of sea anemones. Each one is only about two millimetres across.

Each polyp lives in its own cup-shaped hollow and uses its tentacles to catch food that drifts by.

The polyps are connected by a living layer on the coral surface. Underneath is the hard coral shell, or 'skeleton'.

Box jellyfish

Green sea turtle

Banded coral shrimp

Giant clam
Up to one metre across!

White-tipped reef shark

Parrotfish munch on the soft coral polyps and the hard coral too. They poop out ground-up coral sand, which washes ashore to form sandy beaches.

Coral islands

As a reef builds up and up, it can break the surface of the sea, especially at low tide. Sand collects around the reef, plants start to grow, and eventually it becomes a coral island.

Building a reef

Over many years, generations of coral polyps build more and more layers of coral, creating a large underwater structure – the coral reef. Most coral reefs are made up of many different species of coral, as well as being home to other wildlife. This one is part of the Great Barrier Reef, a long chain of reefs off the coast of Australia.

Clownfish

Butterflyfish

The **mantis shrimp** punches its prey, such as clams and snails, at high speed to break their shells.

Leaping out

Sharks, rays and whales spend their whole lives in the ocean. But occasionally, some of them break free, and spend a few seconds experiencing the fresh air. Then they crash back down with a huge splash! Leaping up out of the sea like this is called breaching.

Pearl divers

In Japan, traditional pearl divers or 'ama', meaning sea women, dive to the seabed to collect pearls, found inside oyster shells, or seafood. They learn to hold their breath for much longer than most people can – sometimes several minutes.

Harbour seal

Harbour seals love to flop around and relax on the shore, but when they're hungry, they dive into the sea to hunt fish and squid, using their flippers to dart, twist and turn. A harbour seal can hold its breath for 30 minutes and dive to 400 m deep!

Taking flight

Flying fish really can fly through the air for long distances! They swim at high speed, launch themselves out of the sea, then glide along above the surface by spreading out their fins. One flying fish was recorded staying in the air for a distance of 400 metres – a 45-second flight!

Hunting birds

A big, fierce fish called the giant trevally has even been seen leaping out of the sea to catch seabirds flying above the water.

Plunging birds

Gannets are big, white seabirds that nest on cliffs. To catch fish to eat, they zoom down from the sky at high speed, plunging into the waves and deep under the water.

Diving in

For most air and land animals, what goes on under the sea is a mystery. Most couldn't survive for long under the waves. But some do enter this watery world just for a while, to feed, bathe or explore.

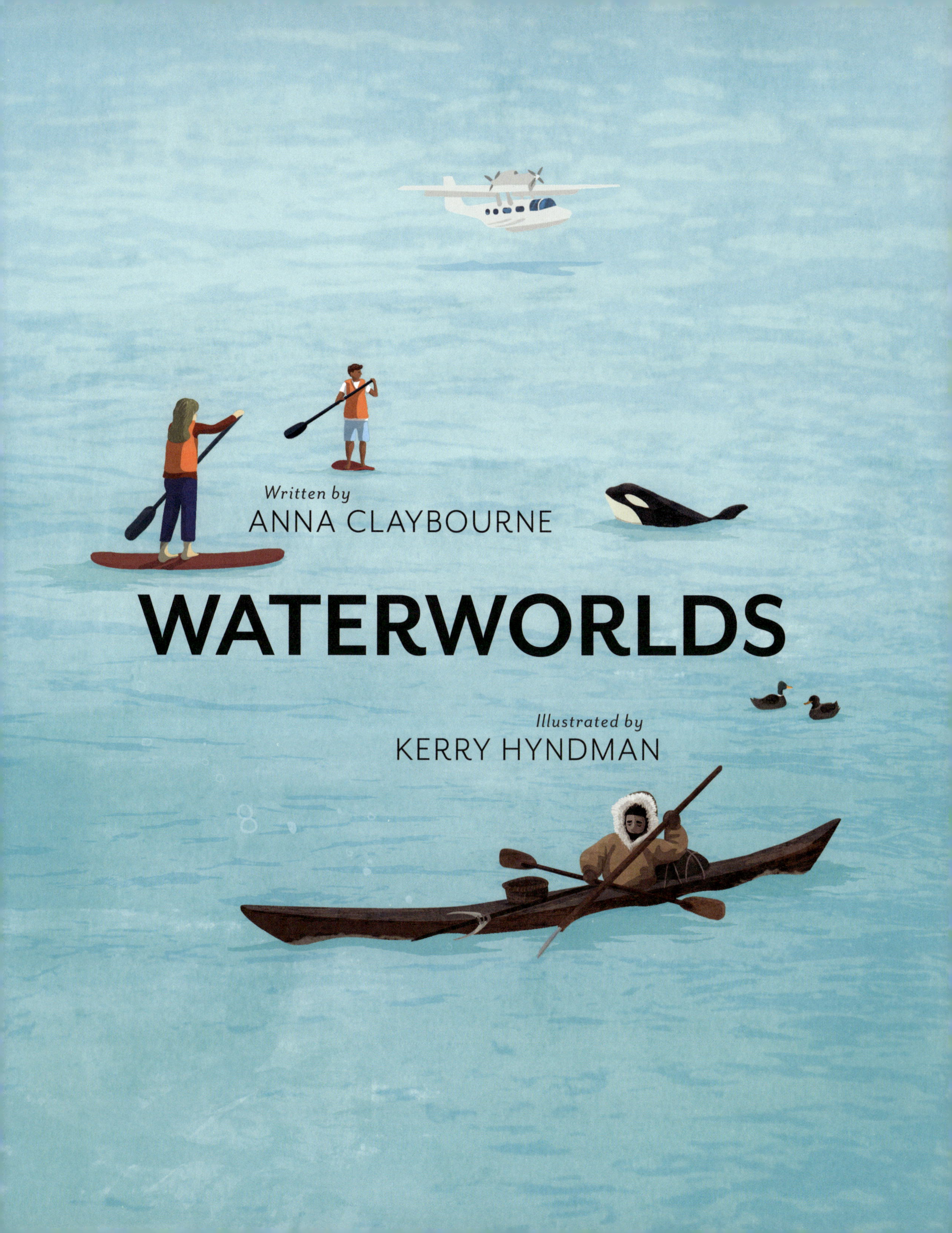

WATERWORLDS

Illustrated by
KERRY HYNDMAN

Written by
ANNA CLAYBOURNE

For Michael.
Anna Claybourne

For Rudy, Eli, Duncan and Juno
Kerry Hyndman

CONTENTS

A world of water — 4
Around and around — 6
Sea stories — 8
Floating boats — 10
Ocean waves — 12
Weather warning! — 14
Rising tides — 16
On the beach — 18
Shaping the shore — 20
Sea levels — 22
Sea ice — 24
Sea power — 26
Sea sports — 28
Life on the surface — 30
Diving in — 32

A world of water

Seen from space, most of our planet, the Earth, looks blue. That's because of the vast seas and oceans that take up almost three-quarters of its surface. They're all connected, forming one huge, endlessly changing seascape, swirling around all the world's land. You could set off by boat from any seashore in the world and sail to any other, if you had enough time!

All day, every day, clouds pile up in the sky, rain falls and streams and rivers rush downhill, carrying water back to the sea in a huge water cycle that keeps our planet alive. Every living thing on Earth, from flowers and trees to elephants, whales, crocodiles and bees, and humans like you and me, needs water too. Without it our world would be a dry, dusty rock, with no life at all.

As water vapour rises higher into the sky, it cools down. This makes it form billions of tiny water droplets. We see them as white, fluffy-looking clouds.

Around and around

The warmer it is, the faster it evaporates.

Water is all around us. As well as filling the seas and oceans, it's in the air, the clouds, the land and inside all living things. It constantly moves around from one place to another, in the water cycle.

Water can be a flowing liquid . . . solid ice . . . or a gas, called water vapour.

At the surface of the sea water evaporates, changing from a liquid into water vapour in the air.

Why is the sea blue?

If you scoop a glass of water out of the sea it doesn't look blue. It looks clear. But as a whole, the sea often looks blue. Sunlight is made up of different wavelengths of light that we see as different colours. The water soaks up – or absorbs – the longer waves of red, orange and yellow light, whereas the shorter blue and greenish light waves bounce around in the water, then bounce back out – so we see a blue-green colour.

. . . and the water is back where it started!

The deeper the water is, the more of the other colours it soaks up, and the bluer it looks.

The wind blows clouds around in the sky. Some blow over the land.

When they get cold, the water droplets clump together to make bigger drops. When they get heavy enough, they fall as rain.

The rain waters the soil, and flows into streams.

The streams connect to make big rivers.

The rivers flow downhill until they reach the sea . . .

WATER CYCLE IN A JAR

You can make your own water cycle inside a jar, and watch these changes happening.

YOU NEED:
A clear, clean glass jar with a lid (such as an old jam jar)
Hot tap water
Ice cubes

1. With an adult to help, fill the jar about 1/4 full with hot tap water.

2. Turn the lid upside down and put it on top of the jar.

3. Put a few ice cubes on the lid.

4. Now watch. Some of the hot water should evaporate, then form a cloud. Where it touches the cold lid, it will form water drops, which fall back down as rain!

Sea stories

The sea is deep, powerful and mysterious, filled with unknown creatures, scary storms and strange sights. Since ancient times, sailors have told fantastical tales of wondrous things they've seen, and there are ocean myths and magical beliefs from all over the world.

Ghost ships

Imagine seeing an eerie phantom ship glowing with light, sailing through the darkness, its ghostly sailors reaching out towards you. Or rowing to the rescue as a ship blazes with fire or gets stuck on a sandbank, only to see it disappear as you come near! Countless people claim to have seen spooky ships like these.

According to legend, the *Flying Dutchman* is a cargo ship from the 1700s that's doomed to roam the ocean forever, never reaching harbour. It appears surrounded by a ghostly glow, and is said to be an omen of disaster or terrible storms.

In Chiloe, an island off the coast of Chile, some say a pale, brightly lit ghost ship appears on foggy nights. Called *El Caleuche*, it's said to be crewed by the ghosts of people lost at sea, or by magical wizards who tempt sailors and fishermen aboard. Some say the ship itself is alive! If you glimpse it you may hear the sounds of music, dancing and laughter, as there's always a party on board.

Since the 1700s, locals have reported seeing a white-sailed ship in the sea, ablaze with fire, in the Northumberland Strait in eastern Canada. People have sometimes sailed towards it to try to help, only for the ship to vanish before their eyes.

Enchanted islands

Can an island hide itself, sink beneath the waves, or only appear once every seven years? Many seafaring tales tell of mysterious islands that behave in strange ways, or are home to magical creatures or fabulous treasures.

HY-BRASIL

Hy-Brasil was a legendary island that often appeared on old maps but was very hard to find, as it could hide in the mist, only revealing itself every seven years. Some said it was the home of Bresal, a great king, and his people, all living forever in great happiness. In the 1600s, a ship's crew claimed to have found and landed on the island – but said they found only one very old magician, and lots of giant black rabbits.

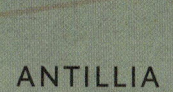

HILDALAND

In the folklore of Scotland's Orkney islands, Hildaland (or 'hidden land') was the summer home of the mermaid-like Finfolk. The beautiful island could sink under the sea to hide from humans.

ANTILLIA

In the 1400s, many people believed that an oddly rectangular island called Antillia lay in the Atlantic Ocean. It was said to have seven great cities, and beaches filled with grains of silver and gold. Some said you could see it from a distance, but it vanished as you came closer.

BUYAN

In Slavic legends of Russia and eastern Europe, the enchanted island of Buyan is the home of the Sun and the east, north and west winds. All weather comes from there, and it's also the home of the Alatyr, the stone at the centre of the universe. However, the island is usually invisible and sailors can never find it.

9

Floating boats

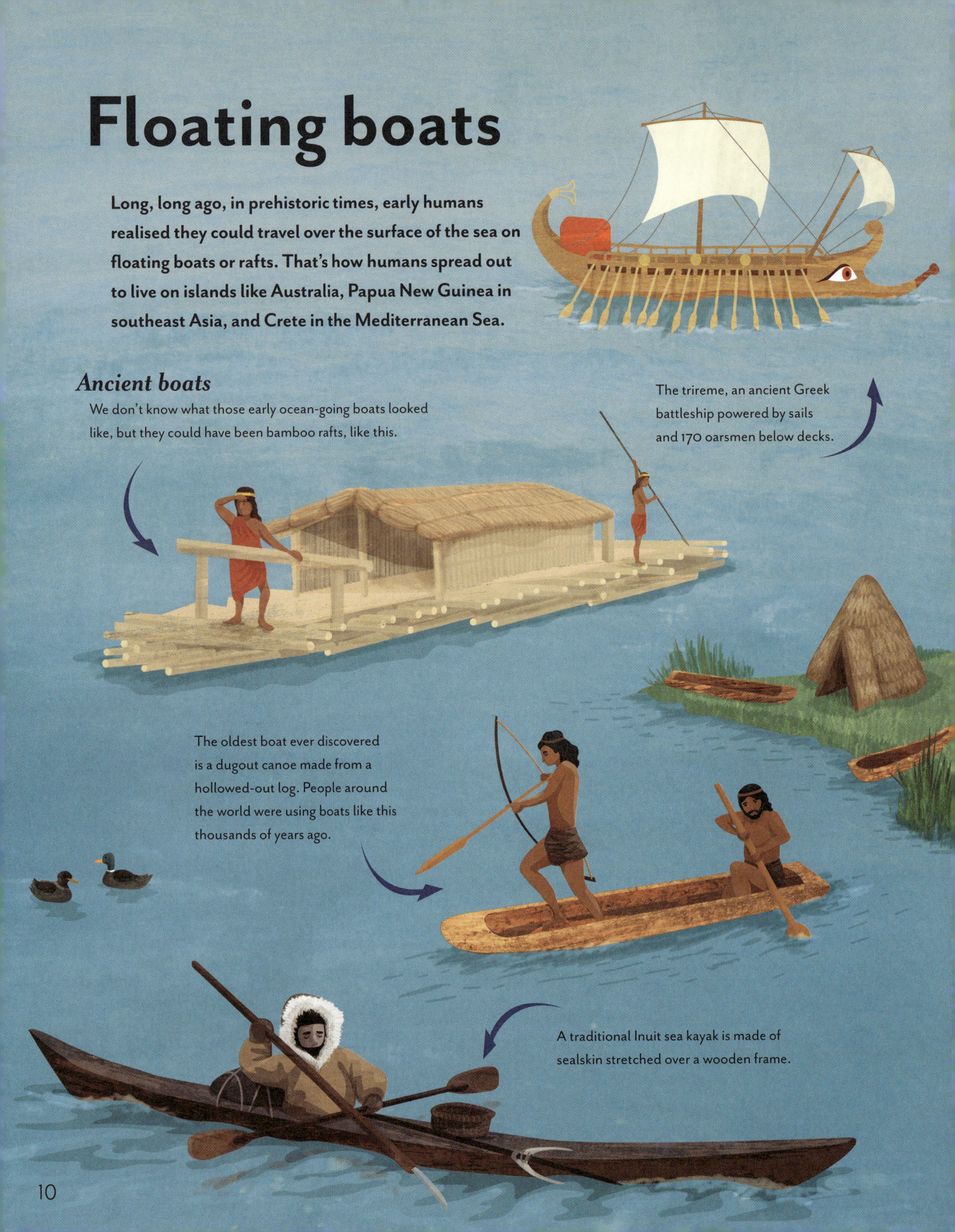

Long, long ago, in prehistoric times, early humans realised they could travel over the surface of the sea on floating boats or rafts. That's how humans spread out to live on islands like Australia, Papua New Guinea in southeast Asia, and Crete in the Mediterranean Sea.

Ancient boats

We don't know what those early ocean-going boats looked like, but they could have been bamboo rafts, like this.

The trireme, an ancient Greek battleship powered by sails and 170 oarsmen below decks.

The oldest boat ever discovered is a dugout canoe made from a hollowed-out log. People around the world were using boats like this thousands of years ago.

A traditional Inuit sea kayak is made of sealskin stretched over a wooden frame.

In the 1700s, pirates used small, fast sailing boats like this sloop to chase treasure-laden ships.

In the 1400s, Chinese explorer Zheng He explored the world in ginormous sailing ships called junks.

Exploring and fighting

The Vikings used wooden longships to explore, carry cargo and invade other lands. Like a trireme, they had both oars and sails.

HOW BOATS FLOAT

Things can float if they are less dense (that is, less heavy for their size) than water. If something is denser than water, such as metal, the water can't hold it up, so it sinks. If it's less dense, like wood, the water pushes up on it and holds it up.

Boats have a shape that traps air inside. This makes them less dense than water, even if they're made of a dense material, like metal.

MAKE A BOAT FLOAT

You can see how this works with some modelling clay.

Drop a solid ball into water, and it sinks . . .

But shape it into a boat with air inside, and it will float!

Boats today

Millionaires cruise the seas in huge high-tech luxury yachts like this.

Massive container ships piled high with containers deliver toys, TVs, clothes and all kinds of other things, all over the globe.

Seaplanes or 'flying boats' can take off from and land on the water.

11

Ocean waves

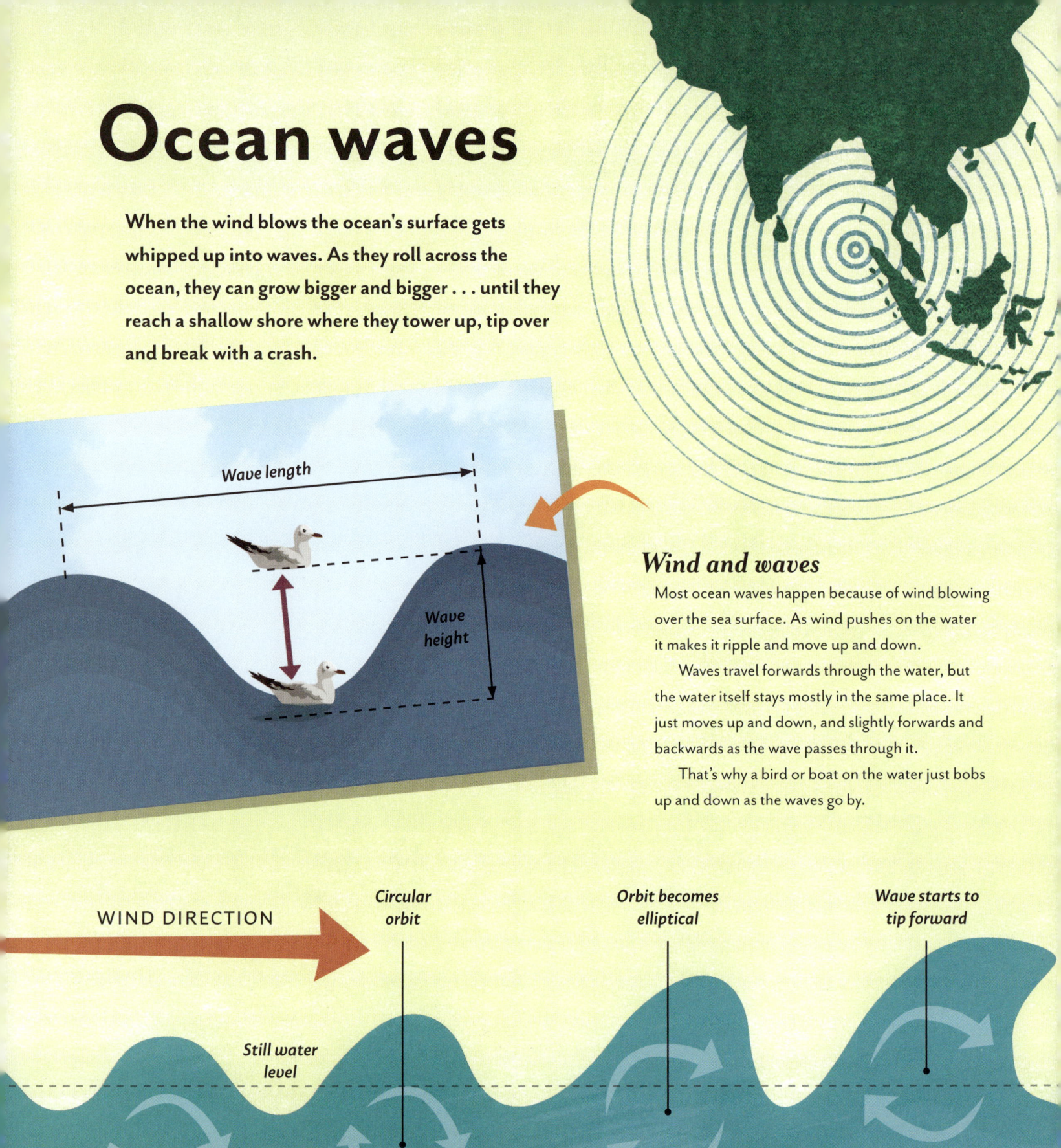

When the wind blows the ocean's surface gets whipped up into waves. As they roll across the ocean, they can grow bigger and bigger . . . until they reach a shallow shore where they tower up, tip over and break with a crash.

Wave length

Wave height

Wind and waves

Most ocean waves happen because of wind blowing over the sea surface. As wind pushes on the water it makes it ripple and move up and down.

Waves travel forwards through the water, but the water itself stays mostly in the same place. It just moves up and down, and slightly forwards and backwards as the wave passes through it.

That's why a bird or boat on the water just bobs up and down as the waves go by.

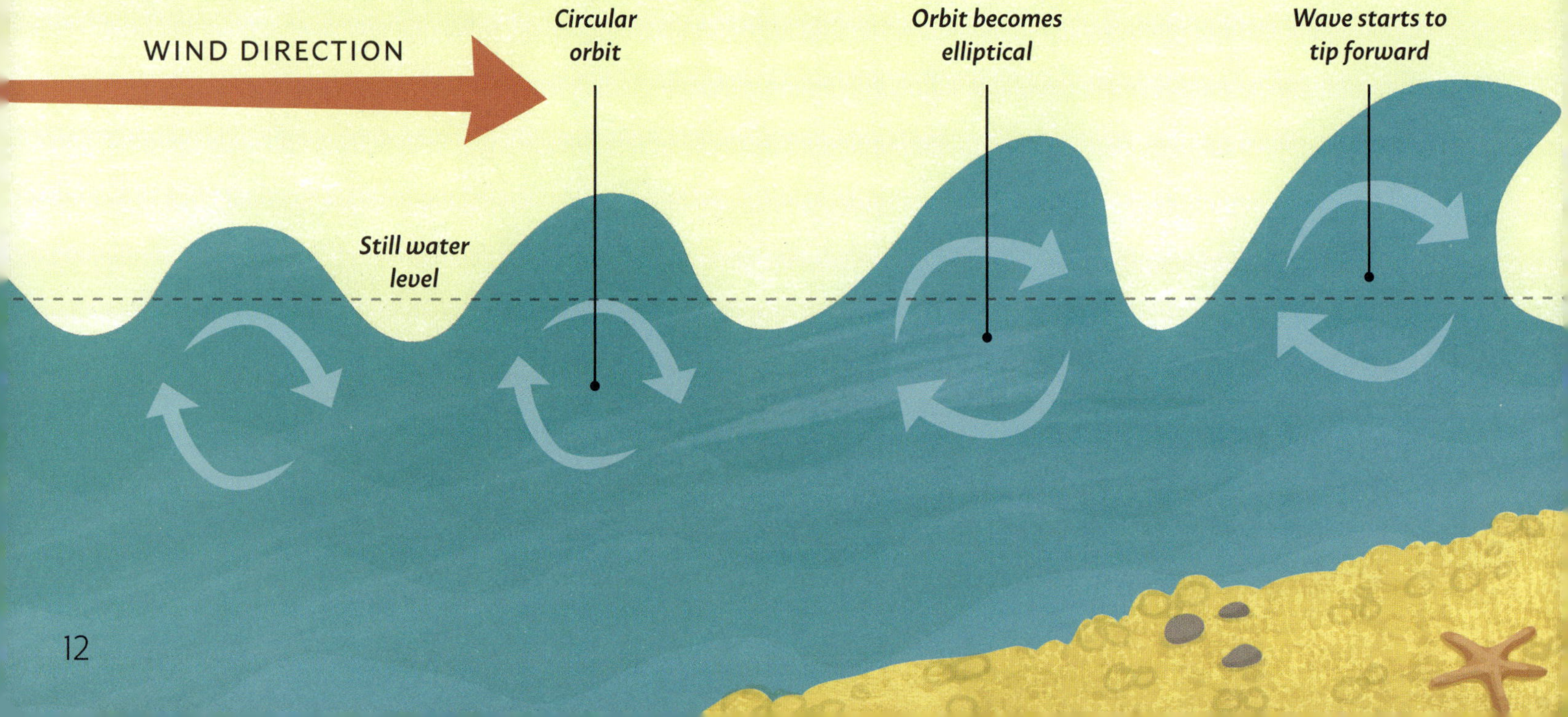

WIND DIRECTION

Circular orbit

Orbit becomes elliptical

Wave starts to tip forward

Still water level

A powerful tsunami in 2004 started near Indonesia and spread out all over the Indian Ocean.

A huge tsunami flowing onto the land in Japan in 2011

WAVES IN A TRAY

Make your own waves in a mini-ocean by filling a large, flat baking tray with water.

- Blow over the water to make waves on the surface.

- Try using a straw to make stronger wind.

Tsunami!

A tsunami is a different kind of wave that can be especially big, and very dangerous.

Tsunamis happen when something makes lots of water move very quickly. It could be an undersea earthquake moving the seabed, or a big landslide slipping down a mountainside into the sea. Just like dropping a pebble into a pond, it makes ripples spread out in every direction. As a tsunami wave approaches the shore, the water piles up and spills onto the land.

BREAKING WAVE

At Nazaré, in Portugal, brave surfers ride giant waves that have travelled thousands of kilometres across the Atlantic Ocean. As they break, they can be over 24 metres tall!

Swash

Backwash

Source of friction

As waves move through shallow water they drag on the seabed, making them tip forwards, curl over and break.

- Drop something into the water, like an eraser or pebble, to make tsunami waves.

- Make an island using modelling clay or a stone. How do tsunami waves travel around the island?

13

Weather warning!

When you're out at sea, one place you don't want to be is in the middle of a raging, roaring ocean storm!

Whirling winds

Tropical cyclones are vast, whirling windstorms that form in tropical parts of the world where the ocean surface is warm. They're sometimes called hurricanes, typhoons or cyclones, depending on where in the world they are.

In the middle is a cloudless, calmer area, the 'eye' of the storm.

Stormy water

The powerful spiralling winds whip up storm waves that can sink or damage even the biggest ships. A ship in a storm is most likely to sink or overturn if a big wave hits it from the side. So ships try to sail straight into the waves, riding through or over them.

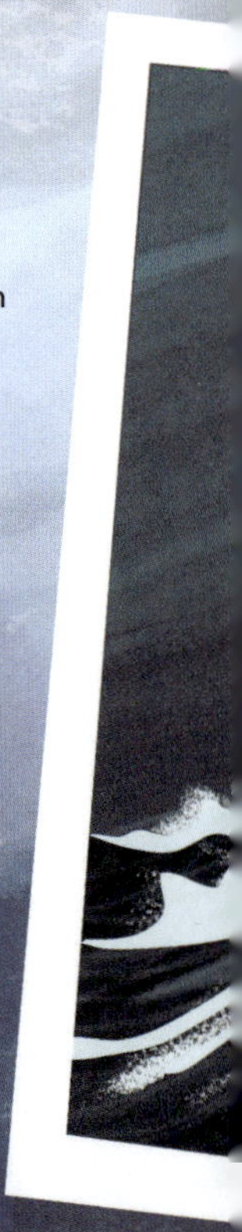

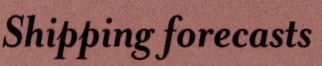

Shipping forecasts

On land, we watch the weather forecast for wherever we live, to see what the weather will bring. Out at sea sailors do the same. They check special shipping forecasts or shipping news broadcasts, using radio signals or satellite internet to help them avoid cyclones, thunder and lightning storms, fog and hail.

Cyclones move as they spin,
eventually reaching the land,
where they can cause big,
dangerous waves, heavy rain
and floods.

Warm, damp air rising
from the ocean surface forms
a spinning mass of clouds.
It can grow to 800 km wide.

Electric glow

Just before or during a lightning storm
at sea, you might see 'St Elmo's fire'
– a strange purplish glow around the
tips of masts, or other pointed parts of
a boat. It's caused by electric charges
building up in the air. Long ago,
sailors thought it was a good omen,
meaning they would get through the
storm safely.

Struck by lightning!

Lightning is a giant electrical spark that can jump
between storm clouds and the ground – or the sea.
Lightning is often drawn towards the highest point in
the area – and a boat on a flat sea is the highest point!
A lightning strike can shatter a yacht's mast,
damage the electrical systems on board a ship, or
even set fire to the boat. Most boats and ships have
a lightning conductor – a strip of metal that sticks up
on top of the mast and runs all the way down into the
water to carry the electricity away safely.

Rising tides

When you build a sandcastle on a sandy beach, you know it won't be there for long. Sooner or later, the tide will come and wash it away.

All over the world, wherever there are seas and oceans, the water rises and falls twice a day with the movement of the tides. But why?

Tide in

The highest tide

In most places, high tide is 1–3 metres higher than low tide. But at the Bay of Fundy in Canada, it can be 16 metres higher! The long, narrow bay channels the rising water into a narrower and narrower space, so it has to rise higher.

Tide out

The flow of the tides and the crashing waves have worn away these rocky stacks, making them narrower at the bottom.

Tides on both sides!

Tides are caused by the Moon's gravity. Though the Moon is smaller than the Earth and a long way away, it still has enough gravity to pull on the world's water. The Moon also pulls slightly on the Earth, and this makes the Earth swing around slightly as the Moon orbits it.

These two forces make the water in the seas and oceans 'bulge' on the side of the Earth nearest the Moon, and on the opposite side too.

High tide

Low tide

Earth

Then as they move away from the bulge, the water falls back down, creating low tide.

High tide

Low tide

Moon

As the Earth itself spins around once every 24 hours, different parts of the sea move into these positions, and their water rises up, leading to high tide.

17

On the beach

What is a beach? It's the bit right next to the sea, between high tide and low tide. Sometimes the beach is underwater and sometimes it's dry land. Scientists call it the 'intertidal zone', and it's home to all kinds of creatures that aren't found anywhere else.

Shorebirds like this plover dig into the sand to catch worms to eat.

Under the sand

When the tide is out, some intertidal creatures go hunting, while others hide under the sand to stay damp.

Lugworms lie in their burrows, swallowing sand and seawater and filtering tiny bits of food out of it. They poo out the uneaten sand, which forms worm-like 'casts' on the beach.

On the rocks

Limpets and barnacles are small sea creatures with shells. Underwater, they come out to feed, but at low tide they close tight, clamped onto the rocks, so they don't dry out.

Barnacles

Keyhole limpet

Solar sea slug

Giant limpet

Small fish

Small, fast-running ghost crabs hide in their holes and pop out to search for food. As soon as you go near them, they pop back in!

There's something else under the sand too – turtle eggs! Sea turtles dig their nests on the beach, lay eggs in them, then cover them over. When the babies hatch, they climb out of the nest and crawl down to the sea.

Life in a rock pool

Rock pools are pockets of seawater that get trapped and left behind on rocky shores when the tide goes out. Small sea creatures can shelter there until the tide comes back in – and some spend their whole lives in rock pools.

What's hiding in this rock pool?

Seaweed

Brittle star (similar to a starfish or sea star)

Sea anemone

Hermit crabs have soft bodies, and use other animals' old shells to hide in.

MAKE A ROCK POOL VIEWER

To get a good look inside, use a rock pool viewer.

YOU NEED:
A large plastic drinks bottle
Strong black or grey packing tape or gaffer tape
Clear food wrap or a small plastic food bag
Elastic bands

1. Ask an adult to cut the top and bottom off the bottle to make a tube.

2. Fold tape over the cut edges, so they're not sharp.

3. Stretch food wrap over one end and use elastic bands to hold it in place.

4. Cover the whole tube with tape (this blocks out light, making it easier to see).

To use the viewer, put it into the water with the window at the bottom, and look into the top.

TAKE CARE!
• Always have a trusted adult with you.
• Only explore shallow rock pools.
• Don't stick your hand in or try to touch the wildlife. They don't like it, and some can sting or nip!

Shaping the shore

Why does the seaside have bays, sandy or pebbly beaches, cliffs and sticking-out headlands? They were all made by the sea over thousands of years, as the tide flowed in and out and the waves crashed against the land.

Creating the coastline

As waves break onto the shore they can slowly wear away or erode the land. Thanks to different types of rocks, this forms a variety of shapes.

Where the land is made of softer rock, it wears away faster, hollowing out a bay.

Beach

Bay

Headland

Where higher land has worn away, you get sea cliffs. The waves weaken the base of the cliff, and every so often another chunk of the cliff falls down – especially during big storms. That's why you shouldn't stand at the edge of a cliff, or right underneath one!

Spectacular shapes

Waves can hollow out deep sea caves under cliffs and make blowholes, where a sea cave connects to a hole in the land above.

Sometimes, waves wear right through a headland, creating an arch

Blowhole

Eventually, an arch can collapse, leaving behind a sea stack

Stacks can end up narrower at the base, where the waves wear them away

When waves rush into the cave at high tide, water shoots up out of the blowhole

20

Spit

Building a beach

Sandy beaches form where gentler waves wash sand, or broken-up seashells or coral, onto the shore. In a sheltered bay the waves are calmer, so beaches form there. Pebbly beaches form from pebbles carried to the coast by rivers, or by glaciers long ago.

A spit is a long, narrow strip of land built by the waves.

In some places, gentler waves deposit sand or mud onto the shore. This can build up extra land.

Harder rock doesn't wear away so fast, so it ends up sticking out and forming a headland. A high headland is a good place for a lighthouse.

Lighthouse

Headland

Washed away!

As wave erosion slowly eats away at cliffs, any houses built on the top get closer and closer to the edge, until they finally fall in. This has always happened, but it's happening faster now, because of climate change. Global warming is making the sea level rise (see page 22) and making some sea storms more powerful, creating higher, bigger waves.

HOMES IN DANGER!

Try this experiment to see how clifftop homes can get washed away.

YOU NEED:
A deep, watertight tray or washing-up bowl
Play sand
Mini houses, such as Monopoly® houses, or just use small erasers or dice.

1. Use tightly packed damp sand to build some land with a cliff edge on one side of the tray. Put your houses on top, near the edge.

2. Carefully pour water into the rest of the tray to make the sea. Make the water level lower than the clifftop.

3. Now use your hand to make waves, pushing the water towards the cliff. How many waves does it take to wash away the houses?

Sea levels

The sea level is the average level of the sea surface all over the world. As all the seas and oceans are linked together, water can flow freely between them, so the level is roughly the same everywhere.

⬜ Glaciers

🟩 Extra areas of land

A map of the world's land and ice cover 20,000 years ago, when the sea level was much lower.

Russia and North America were linked by land in the far north

North America

Britain was joined to mainland Europe (and also mostly covered in ice)

Europe

Atlantic Ocean

Africa

Pacific Ocean

South America

South America was a lot wider

Antarctic

◀ *Sea level*   **The sea level is the height of the surface of the sea.**

22

Changing sea levels

The sea level changes slightly all the time thanks to tides, waves and storms. But what if the sea was a LOT higher or lower? Well, long ago it was!

Around 20–23,000 years ago, the world was going through an Ice Age – an especially cold time in its history. The sea level was much lower, because a lot of the Earth's water was frozen into ice caps, glaciers and snow that covered huge areas of land.

This meant there was much less water in the sea. In fact, the sea level was 125 metres lower than it is now. Lots of areas that are now under the sea were then dry land.

Going up!

The sea level has been much higher in the past too. When the average temperature is warmer, most or even all the world's ice melts, so there's much more water in the sea, and the sea level goes up. 110 million years ago, when the world was very warm, the sea was over 100 m higher than today, and there was a lot less land.

Asia had lots of land that isn't there now

Asia

Pacific Ocean

Indian Ocean

Australia

Australia was much bigger, and connected to Asia

This is what India and Bangladesh would look like if the sea level rose 100 metres. Lots of land would be flooded, and the sea would be much closer to Mount Everest!

Mount Everest

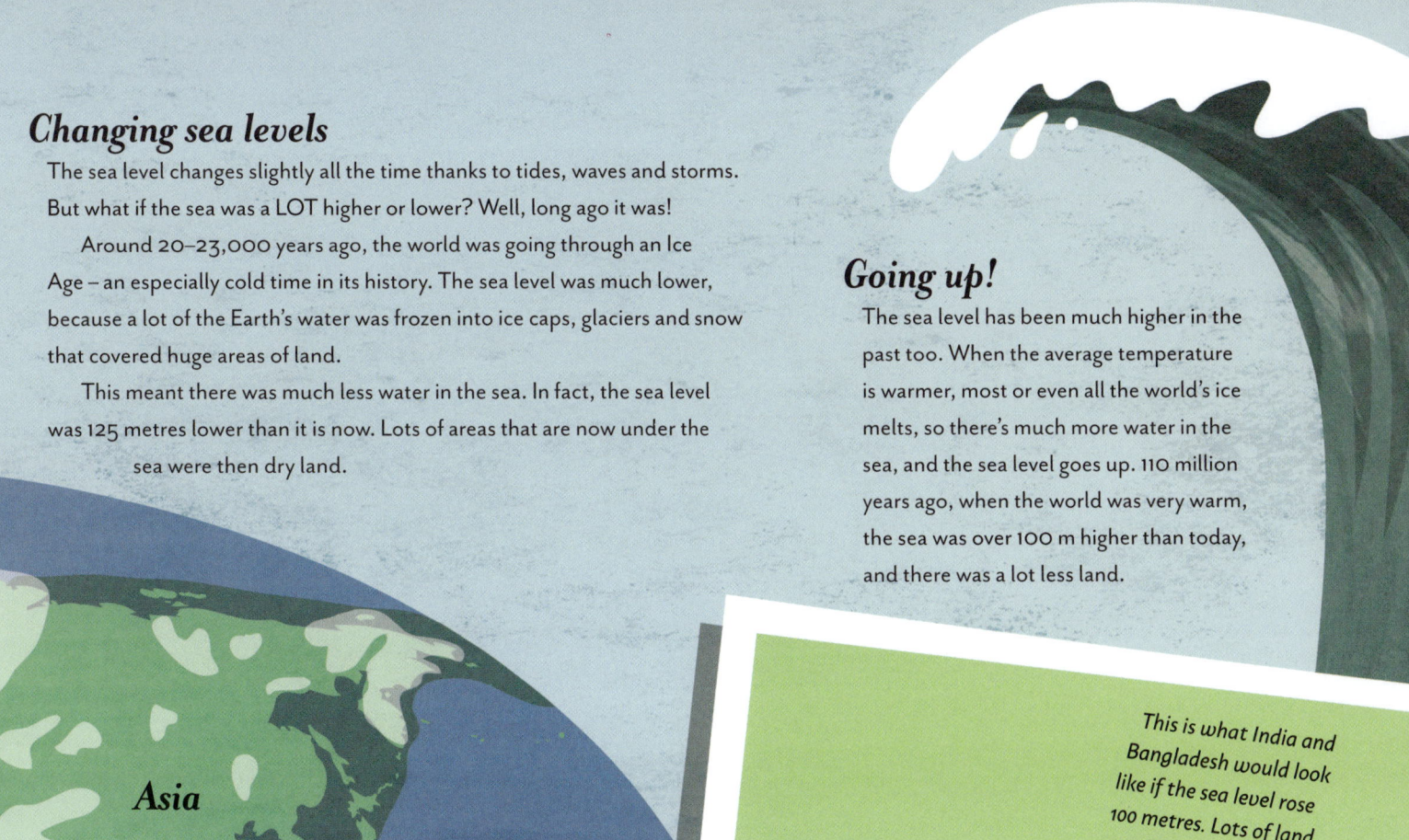

Sea level 100 m

Today, climate change caused by humans is making the world warm up, melting ice and making the sea level rise. If it carries on, it could rise enough to cover some of the world's low-lying coasts and islands.

Sea ice

At the North and South Poles, it's so cold that seawater freezes into solid ice. Sea ice is very important. It reflects the Sun's heat, reducing global warming. Living things like penguins and polar bears rely on it for breeding and hunting. But it can cause disasters too . . .

Like smaller glaciers, the ice sheet slowly moves and flows downhill towards the sea.

The ice cycle

Antarctica at the South Pole, and Greenland near the North Pole, are mostly covered in ice. It falls as snow then packs down to become a hard, solid and VERY thick ice sheet.

At the edges, the shelf cracks and huge chunks break off, forming icebergs. They float away, drifting until they slowly melt.

Ice floats out over the sea, forming a giant ice shelf.

Polar bears use ice floes to hunt seals on!

Algae grows under the ice shelf, providing food for krill, which is then eaten by other animals like seals and whales.

MAKE YOUR OWN ICEBERG

1. To make a mini-iceberg, fill a balloon with water (not too much – just until it's about 10 cm across).
2. Tie it closed, then put it in a small plastic container.
3. Place other objects around it, such as toy bricks or smaller containers, to give it a random shape. 
4. Put it in the freezer (or outside if the weather is below 0°C) to freeze solid.
5. Peel off the balloon to reveal your iceberg!
6. Put it in a large plastic bowl, bucket or sinkful of water to see how it floats.

Anatomy of an iceberg

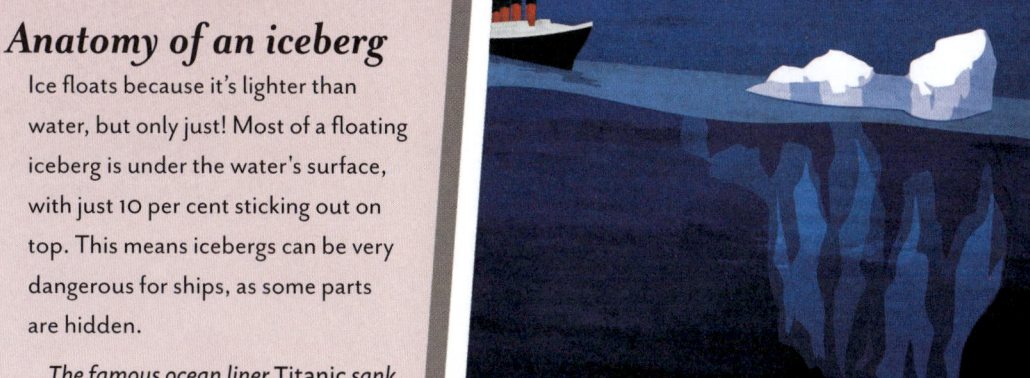

Ice floats because it's lighter than water, but only just! Most of a floating iceberg is under the water's surface, with just 10 per cent sticking out on top. This means icebergs can be very dangerous for ships, as some parts are hidden.

The famous ocean liner Titanic sank after hitting an iceberg in 1912.

Freezing floes

When it's really cold, the sea surface freezes too. This creates flat floating platforms of ice, called ice floes. Seals use ice floes to rest, give birth to pups, or escape from underwater hunters such as orcas.

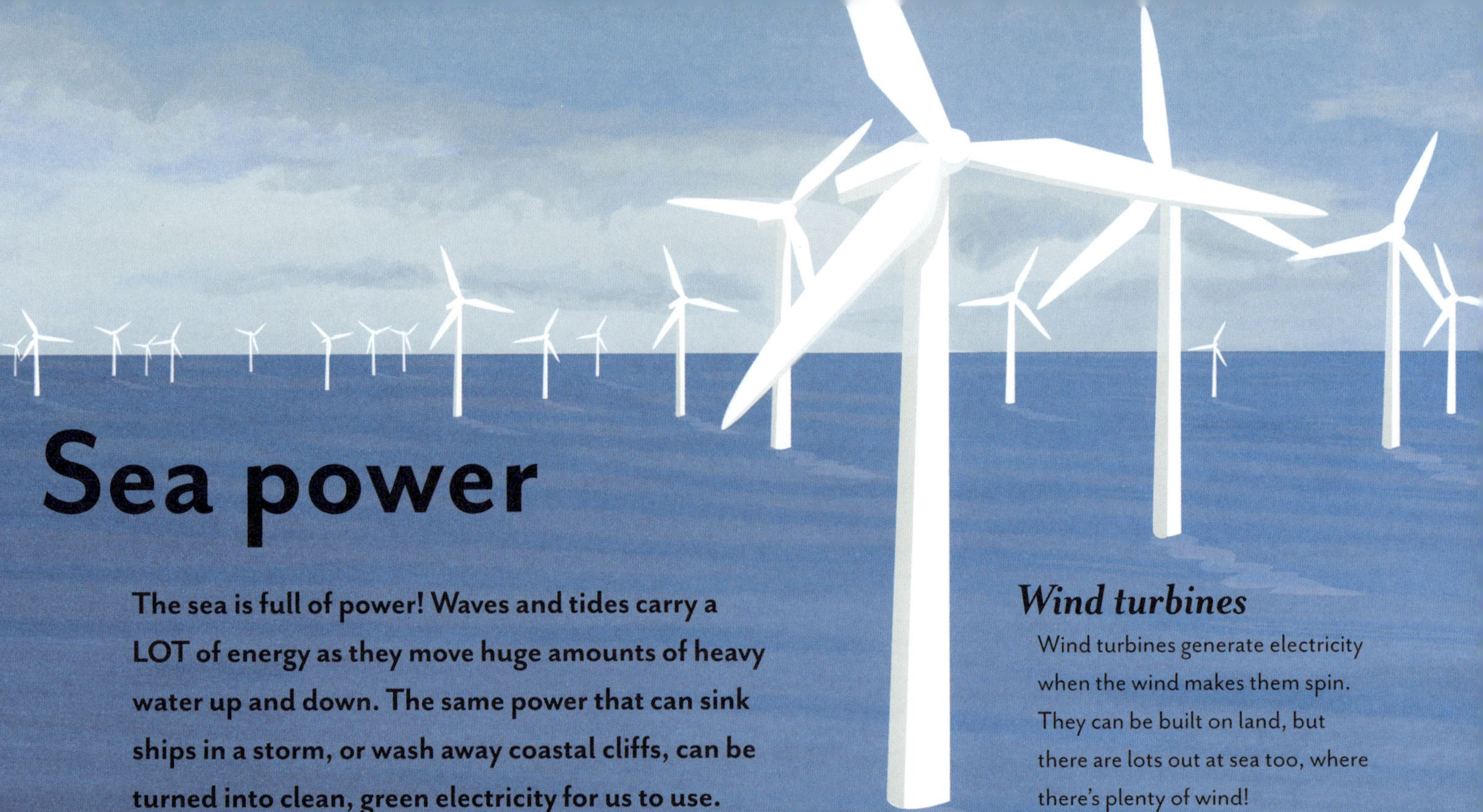

WHY WE NEED IT

We get energy in lots of ways, including burning fuel to power vehicles, heat homes and generate electricity. But burning fuel releases carbon dioxide into the air, and this adds to global warming. Instead, we need to switch to renewable electricity from sources that don't cause pollution, like wind, waves and sunlight, and use electric vehicles and heating.

Sea power

The sea is full of power! Waves and tides carry a LOT of energy as they move huge amounts of heavy water up and down. The same power that can sink ships in a storm, or wash away coastal cliffs, can be turned into clean, green electricity for us to use.

Wind turbines
Wind turbines generate electricity when the wind makes them spin. They can be built on land, but there are lots out at sea too, where there's plenty of wind!

Wave power
Here's one method: a floating wave energy converter. The waves make the floats move up and down. As they move, they turn levers inside the middle section that make turbines spin.

TURBINES

A turbine uses the flow of a liquid or gas to make a wheel spin. A machine called a generator turns the spinning movement into a flow of electricity.

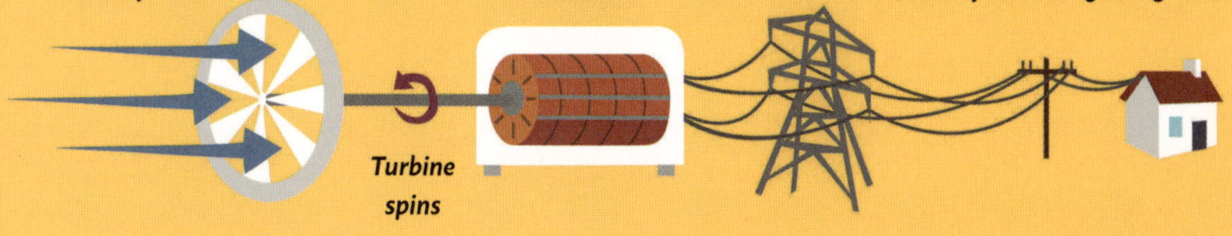

Flow of water → **Turbine spins** → **Generator** → **Flow of electricity along wire**

Energy from the tide

Twice a day, the tide makes the sea rise up and flow in towards the land, then fall back down and flow out. We can capture the energy of these movements with tidal turbines.

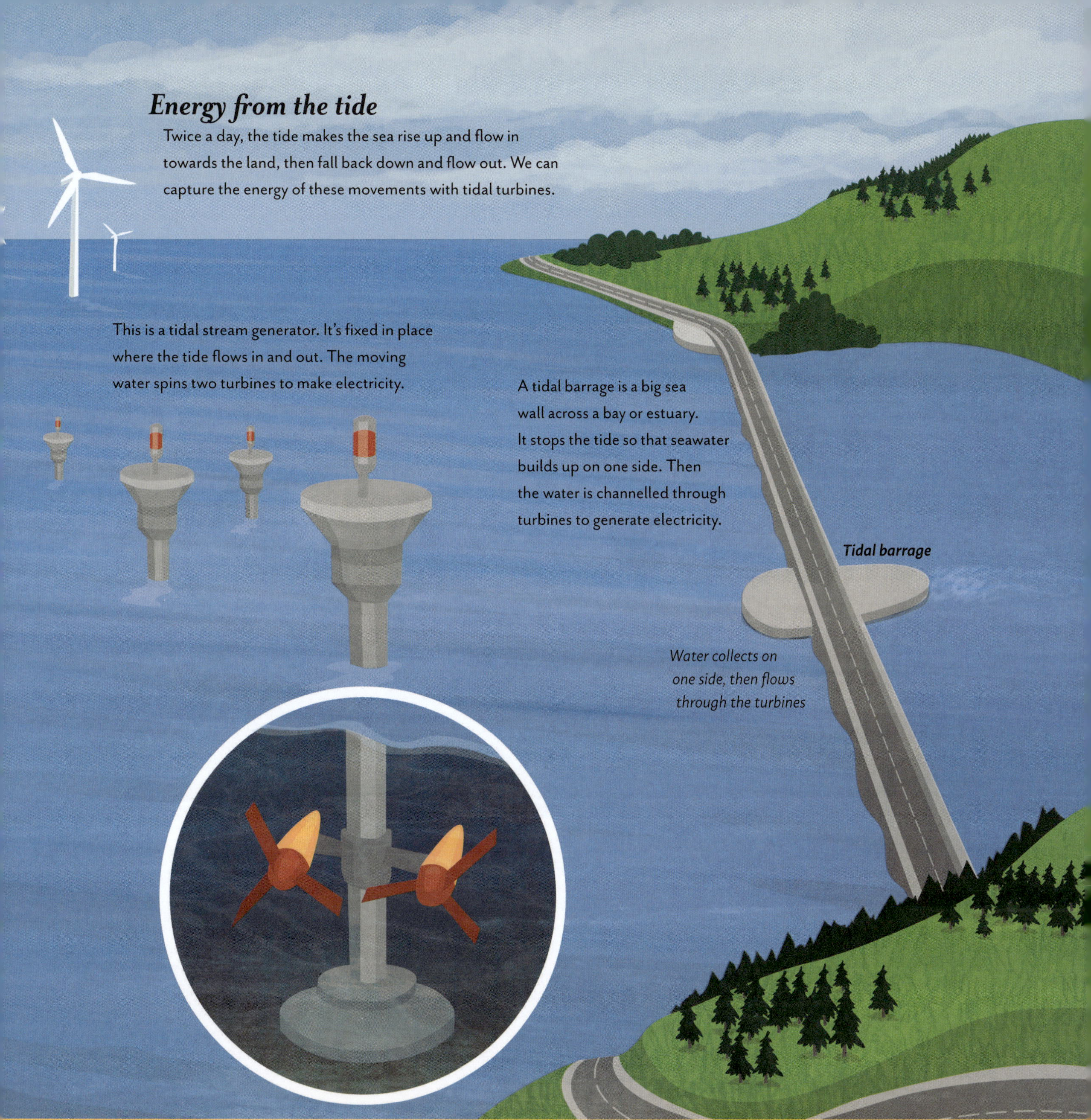

This is a tidal stream generator. It's fixed in place where the tide flows in and out. The moving water spins two turbines to make electricity.

A tidal barrage is a big sea wall across a bay or estuary. It stops the tide so that seawater builds up on one side. Then the water is channelled through turbines to generate electricity.

Tidal barrage

Water collects on one side, then flows through the turbines

27

Sea sports

People go to the seaside to relax, paddle and swim, or do all kinds of exciting sports and activities. Which of these would you love to try?

Surfers ride rolling and breaking waves on floating surfboards.

A jet ski sucks in water and pushes it out at the back in a powerful jet, making the jet ski zoom forward.

...or kitesurf, on a smaller board pulled by a large kite.

You could windsurf, using a surf-style board with a sail...

Fast, high-tech sailing yachts race each other over long distances – or even right around the world.

TAKE CARE!

To avoid crashes, sailors, surfers and others on the water need to keep clear of each other.

Sea kayaking is slower and quieter, so it's a great way to see ocean wildlife.

A lifejacket keeps you afloat if you fall in.

Stand-up paddleboarding is fun and easy to learn.

To go flyboarding, you stand on a board powered by strong water jets. You can zoom up in the air, and dive in and out of the sea like a dolphin!

You can often go parasailing at holiday resorts. You dangle from a parachute that's pulled along by a speedboat.

29

Life on the surface

The seas and oceans are full of wildlife, mostly living underwater. But some plants and animals live on the sea surface. Creatures that live at the surface of the water even have a special name – they're called 'neuston'.

Floating jellies

These floating surface sea creatures are similar to jellyfish, but actually belong to a different animal family, the Hydrozoa. Each one is a community of tiny sea creatures living together, and feeding and moving around like a single animal.

The Portuguese man-o-war or 'blue bottle' floats on the surface thanks to its inflatable sail, while its stinging tentacles grab fish and squid.

Smaller velella, or by-the-wind sailors, feed on plankton. They can form huge shoals of thousands or millions.

The blue button gets its name from its coin-sized round float.

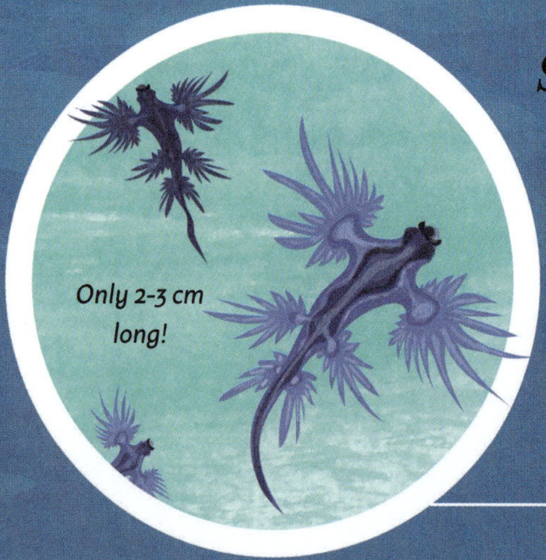

Sea dragons

The amazing blue sea dragon is not a dragon, but a tiny sea slug. It floats upside down on the sea surface, and feeds on other floating creatures such the Portuguese man-o-war. Even though the man-o-war is bigger and has a deadly sting, the sea dragon can hunt it as the sting doesn't affect it. It bites chunks out of its prey and stores its stinging cells in its feathery 'fingers', using them to sting its enemies.

Only 2-3 cm long!

30

TENSION TESTER

How can a sea skater stand on water? It's because of surface tension, which makes water seem to have a stretchy 'skin'. It happens because the molecules water is made of pull towards each other, especially at the surface.

To test it out, try this experiment.

YOU NEED:
A bowl of water
Small metal paperclips, pins or needles
Kitchen paper

1. Try gently placing a paperclip, pin or needle on the water surface. If it's tricky, use the corner of a piece of kitchen paper to lower it onto the surface.

2. Metal objects normally sink, but if they don't break the surface, the surface tension can hold them up. Look closely and you should see dimples in the water where it is being pushed down.

3. If you disturb the water or push the objects down, they'll sink.

There are hardly any sea insects, but the sea skater is one. Like a pond skater, it stands on the surface of the sea, using surface tension to stay up. Its tiny body hairs trap air, creating a mini life jacket that helps the skater pop back up to the surface if it gets swamped by a wave. Sea skaters can be found far out at sea, where they feed on tiny plankton.

The violet snail makes itself a raft of bubbles covered in sticky, snot-like mucus. Then it floats around, feeding on baby Portuguese men-o-war.

Floating seaweed

Sargassum seaweed drifts on the sea surface, using little gas-filled 'bladders' to stay afloat. It provides food and shelter for other sea creatures, like fish, shrimps and baby turtles.

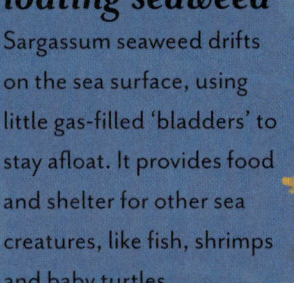

Barnacles filter tiny bits of food out of seawater. Most species cling to rocks or boats, or other animals like whales. But the buoy barnacle clings to a floating object, such as driftwood, or makes its own bubble-filled foam float. Sometimes, lots of buoy barnacles share one float.

Surface birds

Albatrosses are big seabirds that can spend years out at sea. Far from land, they fly low over the waves, and sit on the surface to feed, grabbing octopuses and squid that swim by.

Short-tailed albatross